PURSUING TOTAL QUALITY

101

LOGICAL WAYS

TO

IMPROVE QUALITY

FOR

YOUR CUSTOMERS

(Without Hiring a Guru,

Attending Countless Meetings

or Spending Thousands of Dollars)

■

DICK SCHAAF/MARGARET KAETER

Lakewood
Publications
A Maclean Hunter Company

QUANTITY SALES

Most Lakewood Books are available at special quantity discounts when purchased in bulk by companies, organizations and special interest groups. Custom imprinting or excerpting can also be done to fit special needs. For details write: Lakewood Books, 50 South Ninth Street, Minneapolis, MN 55402 or call (612) 333-0471.

∎

LAKEWOOD BOOKS
50 South Ninth Street
Minneapolis, MN 55402
(612) 333-0471; Fax: (612) 333-6526

Publisher: Philip Jones
Production Manager: Brenda Owens
Designer: Kathleen Timmerman

10 9 8 7 6 5 4 3 2 1

Lakewood Publications Inc. is a subsidiary of Maclean Hunter Publishing Company. Lakewood publishes TRAINING Magazine, The Quality Imperative Magazine, The Training Directors' Forum Newsletter, Creative Training Techniques Newsletter, The Service Edge Newsletter, Total Quality Newsletter, Potentials In Marketing Magazine, Recreation Resources Magazine and other business periodicals and books.

Dick Schaaf and Margaret Kaeter, Vernacular Engineering, P.O. Box 19316, Minneapolis, MN 55419; (612) 435-3630.

ISBN 0-943210-22-4

CONTENTS

Before Engaging In Hot Pursuit

WE HAVE A LITTLE PROBLEM WITH THE IDEA of TOTAL QUALITY. That's how it's said these days—as though suddenly we're talking in CAPITAL LETTERS so everyone can see how REALLY IMPORTANT we consider this TOTAL QUALITY stuff to be.

"Total" Quality?

Is there another kind? Quality Monday through Thursday afternoon, but Fridays we phone it in? Quality when the moon is in the first to third quarters, so long as Jupiter doesn't align with Mars? Quality for now, until we come up with something new to put on the banners and buttons?

Semantics aside, the idea of TOTAL QUALITY carries with it a sense that, in our own peculiarly American way, we're once again looking for One Big Answer, one silver bullet that will make everything all right forever.

We think not. We tend to think in pieces and parts rather than totalities. Years ago, Jan Carlzon of Scandinavian Airlines System (SAS) explained the service-focused transformation of what had been a struggling airline into one of the world's premier carriers by observing that SAS never started out to get 100 percent better at any one thing—it decided to get one percent better at 100 different things.

That's our mindset. Only we take his logic one step farther: 101 different things.

In the pages that follow, we've tried to break the TOTAL QUALITY challenge into an understandable, manageable subset of component parts. Taken individually, none of them will make everything all right forever. But selected for their relevance and combined for their impact, we believe they can make things a whole lot better for the time being—and should, indeed, inspire still further continuous improvements.

That's what the quality "movement" consists of. Continuous improvements. Incremental changes. Little

1

steps that, over time, get you where you're going. After which, you go someplace else. The journey never ends.

So if you're going to dedicate yourself to pursuing TOTAL QUALITY, we hope you'll go about it in a realistic, orderly, systematic fashion. One step at a time. A combination of a variety of activities, not an unreasoning quest for One Big Important Solution.

But if you accept that kind of slow and steady approach, be prepared to follow a moving target. Be willing to buy in to futurist Alvin Toffler's idea that we have to develop an ability to "learn, unlearn and relearn" as a matter of course.

And have a little fun while you're at it. Sure, this is work. But it's work we can be good at. It's work that gives us back our hands, that allows us to leave fingerprints all over what we're doing. In case you're wondering, you leave fingerprints the same way you did when you were five years old. You get your hands dirty. Then you touch places where you can leave an impression—something that can be seen and appreciated by someone who's really important. Your customer.

After all, TOTAL QUALITY is really for the customer. That's the underlying point and purpose of the continuous improvements we're all working so hard to make. Making customers happy. Making them happy they chose to do business with you. Making them happy they believed in your quality commitment enough to risk their own precious time and money. Making them so happy that they want to come back and repeat the experience of being your customer again and again.

TOTAL QUALITY is for OUR CUSTOMERS.

That's what this book is all about.

Dick Schaaf and Margaret Kaeter
Burnsville, MN
June 2, 1992

Chapter 1

Master The Basics

YOU LEARNED TO CRAWL BEFORE YOU BEGAN TO WALK, to walk before you could run. Quality movements benefit from similar progressions—and can require similar amounts of time to grow from the first hesitant steps to true coordination and stamina. Don't rush into yet another bold new program before you've developed the essential skills.

1 / Hire A Baldrige Consultant—On Paper

2 / Skew The Baldrige

3 / Kill The Inspectors

4 / Reduce (or Increase) Variation

5 / Eliminate Fear

6 / Cut Cycle Time

7 / Focus On Today, Not Tomorrow

8 / Prepare To Succeed

9 / Explain Quality Decisions

10 / Just Do It

Hire A Baldrige Consultant — On Paper

THE MALCOLM BALDRIGE NATIONAL QUALITY AWARD is so much more than a piece of corporate crystal. It's a complex, far-reaching, highly detailed process for breaking the big challenge of quality into a thousand different pieces, a basic language and template for getting into continuous quality improvement. In other words, it's a tool. As any proud craftsperson will tell you, don't scrimp on tools. Pick good ones, then use them to their utmost potential. Forget the Baldrige *Award*. It's the process that gives you a way of coming to grips with the many facets of the quality challenge. Use it as a tool, not a goal.

At tiny Steinwall, Inc., a plastics manufacturer in the Minneapolis suburb of Fridley, the Baldrige criteria and those developed for the Minnesota Quality Award, a state-level counterpoint, are viewed as a form of consulting expertise. Maureen Steinwall, owner of the 60-person firm, reasons that she could ill afford to acquire such expertise from megabuck consultants. But the processes all those experts have created are readily available and easy to apply.

Skew The Baldrige

THE BALDRIGE AWARD PROCESS HAS DONE WONDERS IN focusing the attention of American business on quality (especially top management folks whose competitive juices have been brought to a boil by the prospect of a trophy for the corporate mantelpiece). In the process, unfortunately, the whole thing has started to take on some of the trappings of a cult, its good intentions distorted in ways never intended by its originators. Companies now pronounce the mindless mantra, "going for the Baldrige," as if it somehow evidences intelligence, sanctity and commitment.

The Baldrige criteria didn't come down off a mountain etched on stone tablets. In fact, they change constantly as the people charged with administering the Baldrige process pursue their own form of continuous improvement. What they do, you should too. To the extent that the Baldrige criteria serve the needs of your business—and especially the needs of your customers—use them as guidelines for your quality efforts. In those areas where your own efforts are already stronger or better focused, be true to yourself. Don't sacrifice a strength for an award.

Kill The Inspectors

FIGURATIVELY SPEAKING, OF COURSE. THE TRADITIONAL approach to quality has been to "inspect it in" by creating specific jobs, even entire departments, to examine things after they're done and approve or reject their quality. In some companies, as many as half the people on the payroll are primarily involved in inspecting the quality of someone else's work. (If you're a manager, be honest: How much of your time is devoted to reviewing and endorsing, or kicking back, the work of your subordinates?)

The key to dismantling what Armand Feigenbaum aptly labeled the "invisible factory" is to identify inspection steps on the back end that can be incorporated into the activities of people throughout the process. Boston's Beth Israel Hospital pioneered the idea of primary nursing care, empowering frontline nurses to develop personalized patient care plans—and eliminated two tiers of management in the process. At the 3M computer products plant in Weatherford, OK, *anyone* who spots bad product in the making shuts down the line until the problem is corrected.

Reduce (or Increase) Variation

QUALITY OFTEN MEANS CONSISTENCY. IN SIMPLISTIC terms, the more consistency, the greater the perceived quality. The more inconsistency, the more the customer can become confused, disoriented, disgruntled, perhaps ultimately an ex-customer. Consequently, a good deal of quality activity aims to reduce variation. Variation has causes. Always. Some causes are normal. Some are abnormal. To improve quality, you have to know the difference—normal causes can be addressed by continuous quality improvement efforts; abnormal ones can't.

That means looking closely at every facet of your operations. Perdue Farms, the East Coast chicken producer, achieves greater product consistency by putting all birds through the required USDA inspections plus another 23 to 31 tests. Motorola has now moved beyond driving defects below 3.4 per million. Atlanta-based Shop'n Chek deploys its national network of mystery shoppers to evaluate a client's employees as they handle sales-inducing interactions with customers. But remember that quality is what the customer says it is—and in many service businesses today, the customer *is* the variation in the process. If the customer wants variation, that's what you have to manage for.

Eliminate Fear

W. EDWARDS DEMING HAS BEEN PREACHING THIS ONE for 50 years now. So who could be against quality? Anyone who has been burned by any predecessor, that's who. The residue of decades of false starts, empty promises, rancorous labor relations and management styles that too often have protected perks and turf at the top is a healthy skepticism throughout the organization. As soon as people get punished, belittled, made even the tiniest bit queasy—or work themselves out of a job—in their efforts to embrace the new directive, everyone learns not to try that again.

United Air Lines eliminates fear by having employees and their supervisors sign pledges that no one will ever be punished for their efforts to solve a customer's problem. Federal Express goes a step farther with its Guaranteed Fair Treatment Process, which lets employees who feel they've been wronged appeal the decision through their own chain of command, ultimately all the way to an appeals board composed of the CEO, the COO and other top executives. Might doesn't make right. It makes fear.

Cut Cycle Time

"SPEED IS LIFE," ARGUES TOM PETERS. DISCOVER WAYS TO deliver faster and you've mastered a basic component of quality improvement. Even if speed isn't yet a major issue with the customer, streamlining your processes builds natural time and cost efficiencies that can help you meet even greater customer needs in the future— and operate more profitably today.

At Fidelity Investments, the largest mutual fund company in the world, a top priority is getting checks from investors to the bank so fund managers can put the money to work. Since Fidelity's trucks transport checks 24 hours a day, 60% of funds received the previous day are deposited by 9 a.m. In one recent year, rushing the money to the bank earned an extra $20 million in interest for Fidelity customers. It used to take the accountant at Minnesota-based Johnson Filtration Systems several days to prepare more than 20 reports at the end of each reporting period. Today, he prepares one consolidated report, puts it in a three-ring binder and circulates it. And guess what? Readership is up because of the reduced time needed to handle the information.

7

Focus On Today, Not Tomorrow

DON EPHLIN IS A FORMER VICE PRESIDENT OF THE
United Auto Workers who took part in the beginnings
of the quality transformation at Ford and the birth of
General Motors' Saturn venture. He remembers that at
his first meeting as a new member of GM's internal
Quality Council, the discussion focused almost entirely
on new models planned for the following year. Asked
whether he wasn't excited to be given a peak at the
company's future, his response was astonished disbe-
lief. The problems, he responded, are here today. And
they won't wait for the next model year.

Grand plans and ambitious objectives have their
place in creating a vision of the organization's future.
But talking about the wondrous developments to be re-
alized on the horizon won't get the bridge built across
the chasm that separates where the organization is today from that bright, beckoning future. Focus on the
individual, unglamorous but essential steps that have to
be taken. Otherwise, the "quality journey" will never
get anywhere.

Prepare To Succeed

ACCORDING TO ZENGER MILLER, A SAN JOSE, CA-BASED consulting firm, the basic reason companies fail to achieve their quality goals is that they start their efforts *before* their people have the skills to make them happen. People who understand the goals of quality theory, but don't have the skills to apply the theory to the practical, everyday realities of their own jobs, consistently fail to meet organizational objectives. It has nothing to do with commitment. It has everything to do with competence.

The tools of quality range from the "Basic Seven" —check sheets, scattergrams, histograms, run charts, control charts, cause-and-effect diagrams (sometimes called fishbone or Ishikawa diagrams) and Pareto diagrams—to highly specialized ways to measure and control highly specific processes and conditions. Make sure your people know not only *how* to use the tools capably, but more importantly *when* to use which one. And don't overlook the way quality tools are being built into continually improving computer software. It's the Information Age's equivalent of power tools.

Explain Quality Decisions

EVEN AFTER BEING TRAINED IN FISHBONE ANALYSIS, THE ultimate why answerer, most organizations stop asking questions way too soon. We've heard at least one claim that the only way to discover if you've truly found the answer to a problem is to set a goal of asking why 100 times. If that raises the prospect of dealing with the equivalent of the two-year-old who drives us crazy with a constant stream of why questions, remember that your people aren't two-year-olds (though many of them probably feel they've been treated as such from time to time).

A basic premise of any quality improvement effort is that it must include all aspects of operations. There are no sacred cows where quality is concerned. It follows that whatever it is, and whoever is doing it, people should always be encouraged to ask why. Then ask why again. And those questions should be indulged, considered and answered—to the questioner's satisfaction. Too often, we're too quick to come up with a simple answer that we think resolves even the most complex problems. If they still have questions, you still have some explaining to do.

10

Just Do It

THE LAST TIME WE FLIRTED WITH QUALITY, WE SPENT too much time running around in "circles" and never got anywhere. Companies with only a superficial commitment to improvement formed Quality Circles that ate up hours of time and gallons of sweat equity, but typically turned out to be little more than a corporate dallying (or delaying) tactic. Quality improvement requires thought, but the thought must lead to substantive action or nothing will change.

At General Electric, formal, long-term quality efforts are teamed with a program of "Work-Out" meetings, patterned after New England town meetings. Employees representing all levels of the business at hand meet periodically to discuss ways to improve the company. On the third day, the group presents recommendations to top management and receives an immediate yes, no or request for more information—with a response promised in a specific time. Even decisions involving millions of dollars are often made quickly when the group can present a good case.

CHAPTER 2

Delight The Customer

QUALITY IS FOR CUSTOMERS. THAT'S THE POINT. THAT'S the purpose. The act and the art of being in business today is the act and the art of having customers. And not just once. The best customer to have is one you've already got. Work to develop long-term quality relationships and you'll bring customers back again and again. That's where the money is.

Know Your Customers

CUSTOMERS ARE A KEY SOURCE OF VARIATION IN THE process, so the more you know about them, the more consistent and satisfying a job you can do on their behalf. Use every means at your disposal to improve your customer IQ. Survey customers regularly. Bring them together in one-time focus groups or continuing advisory panels. Poll your salespeople, the technical service department, the behind-the-scenes people in the back office for feedback on their customers' ever-changing needs and expectations.

Use small instruments as well as large ones. Consider, for example, the lowly comment card. A few questions, a few numbers to circle, space for a cryptic note at the bottom. Each Marriott hotel property is expected to generate a quota of comment cards to provide a continuing overview of guest satisfaction. Emerald People's Utility District in Oregon incorporates a feedback panel into every monthly bill. Alone, they're far from scientific measures of customer satisfaction. But they can point the way for (and validate the findings of) more formal continuing research, provide a barometric reading on products and services, highlight superior or poor employee performance and give insight into myriad other concerns.

Understand Customer Loyalty

CUSTOMERS, WHETHER DOING BUSINESS AS CONSUMERS or business-to-business, have a selfish interest in developing proven vendor relationships: It's complicated, time-consuming and often far from satisfying to continually be looking for new suppliers when there's an old faithful attentively near at hand whose quality is a given. If you're keeping tabs on your customers, you won't be surprised to see them come back again (and you'll spot and eliminate the kindling of minor problems before the bridge gets burned).

To build competitive niches for its products, 3M focuses on FABs: features, advantages and benefits. Features include every aspect of the product, from the reliability and quality of individual components to supportive elements such as customer service. Advantages directly relate to the product's performance against the competition—3M typically subordinates pricing issues to quality, durability, reliability and compatibility with other products and systems. Benefits are what the customer can gain by choosing one product over another. The objective is to align the FABs with long-term customer needs to bring that customer back again and again. That's where the long-term profits lie.

Manage Expectations

CUSTOMER EXPECTATIONS ARE CRUCIAL TO CUSTOMER satisfaction. And many, if not most, of your customer's expectations you can set or modify. Use that power wisely. When you promise something by a certain date or time, your customers expect that you know you can deliver. When you don't, not only have you kept them waiting, you've also given them a reason to question your control of the quality of your products and processes. That's when they start looking for other suppliers.

If you say you're going to return the call, deliver the project or solve the problem by noon, do it. If you can't, don't make a promise you're not going to be able to keep. Remember, though, that customers are often a lot more understanding than we give them credit for. Consider the airline industry, for example: On-time arrivals are up, and with them customer satisfaction ratings. Is that because they're flying faster? No. They've systematically padded their schedules to allow for the inevitable delays that are facts of life in the system. As passengers, we could care less how long the flight lasts. We just care when it ends.

Target Zero Defections

WHY NOT? THE TIME-HONORED RULE OF THUMB IS THAT it takes five times as much money to acquire a new customer as it does to keep one you already have. Data from industry after industry clearly show a pattern of increasing profitability as customer accounts mature beyond the first year or two of learning the products and services and settle into long-term buying patterns. Employees from the sales force to the back office know it's easier to take care of customers whose peculiarities are known and understood than to guesstimate how to satisfy a new account.

Learn how to calculate some meaningful new numbers: defection rates (how many customers stop doing business with you, and why) and lifetime value (the amount of money customers will spend with you if they remain loyal). Putting the two together provides a cost factor for lost customers—and the numbers can be breathtaking. According to Frederick Reichheld and W. Earl Sasser, Jr., writing in the *Harvard Business Review*, a 2% improvement in customer loyalty often yields the same bottomline results as a 10% across-the-board cost reduction.

Sell With Quality

ACCORDING TO LEARNING INTERNATIONAL, A STAMFORD, CT, consulting firm, the odds that a company today is "into quality" are better than 50-50. But the odds of that quality movement involving the organization's sales force are only about one in 10. Yet no process is more vital to the long-term health and vitality of the business than the process of finding, retaining and building loyalty in customers.

Bringing quality to sales means changing the tools by which the process has traditionally been managed. Becoming process, not detail, oriented. Working toward long-term, not short-term, objectives. Rewarding for customer retention, not just customer acquisition. Emphasizing client knowledge, not just product knowledge. Compensating based on partnerships, not quotas. It also means giving salespeople knowledge of quality tools so they can map their processes, analyze their steps and refocus their activities in ways that help themselves and the business succeed. To make sure its sales force stays focused on customer-oriented quality, Hewlett-Packard includes quality and satisfaction measures in compensation equations.

Sell With Quality People

A 1989 STUDY OF CUSTOMER LOYALTY CONDUCTED BY Learning International shows just how important salespeople are to quality outcomes. In a survey of 210 customers in seven industries, actual product performance—the typical focus, at least initially, of many manufacturing-based quality improvement efforts—placed a distant fourth among six factors that influence buying decisions.

The top three characteristics, on the other hand, all involved the salesperson's contributions to the process of creating a viable partnership: their business expertise, their problem-solving skills and their ability to satisfy customer needs before, during and after the sale. Taken together, these three aspects of the selling process account for a weighted factor of 77% of the buyer-seller relationship. Your salespeople have the crucial job of educating your customers to the quality of the products and services you're in business to provide. Make sure they're fully prepared to do that, then support them in every way you can.

Learn From The Competition's Customers

WHEN FORD WAS DEVELOPING THE MID-RANGE TAURUS, it didn't ask customers what they liked and disliked about current mid-range Ford products. Instead, it asked customers of Mercedes-Benz, BMW and other luxury car makers what *they* liked about those vehicles. Then it took more than 80 characteristics of these luxury cars and built them into a new model designed for a far-from-luxury buyer. The Taurus, and the customer focus behind it, led the revival of Detroit's long-time #2 auto company.

Honda used the same tactic in laying the groundwork for a new nameplate that would at once raise its profile in the U.S. market and allow it to get around import quotas. Instead of assuming what the American car-buying public needed from a new model line, Honda examined every other automotive company doing business in the U.S., analyzing the niche each held, its specific strengths in both products and services, and its demonstrated weaknesses as seen by customers. The result was a competitively priced luxury car designed to fill a previously-unsuspected quality niche in every area from reliability to customer service. Acura.

Make Customer Service A Profession

REMEMBER THE DAYS WHEN CUSTOMER SERVICE WAS AN entry-level job? "Here are the rules and there are the angry customers . . . explain the rules to them." Today's successful companies are turning that scene around, making their customer service departments attractive, rewarding and career-advancing places to work, and employing seasoned professionals with experience and training in skills from creative problem solving to information management.

In recent years, Tennant Co., a quality-obsessed manufacturer of floor maintenance equipment, has expanded the customer relations department from six to 34 employees, increasing salaries to as much as $30,000. Starting qualifications now include at least two years of college plus two years of customer service experience—or five years of experience. The result? Service reps with an aptitude for quickly finding technical information in reams of reference materials plus the interpersonal skills to communicate it effectively. Professionals.

Listen To Your People

CAN'T ALWAYS FIGURE OUT WHAT YOUR CONSTANTLY changing customer base wants on a day-to-day basis? Can't afford a continuous program of customer surveys or focus groups? Want new products and services that your customers will immediately notice? Try asking your frontline employees what they hear from customers. They know your customers and your systems in intimate detail, from the joy of hearing a customer marvel at the quality of the company's activities to the frustration of explaining why they can't deliver a desired product or service (even though XYZ Corp. right down the block can and does).

Northwestern Mutual Life Insurance Co. puts sales agents on the corporate committees that review new products and procedures, modify existing offerings and help the company stay in touch with policyholders. Group Health, Minnesota's largest HMO, has changed patient scheduling procedures based on receptionists' reports of customer complaints. Dain Bosworth, a regional brokerage firm, frequently alters its investment offerings after polling its registered reps for customer requests.

Put Managers In The Customer Loop

AT FIRST NATIONAL BANK OF CHICAGO, THE STANDARD is to serve 95% of customers (walk-in traffic averages nearly 200,000 per month) in less than five minutes. That's an impressive statistic for any bank, and it didn't come about by increasing productivity at the frontline. Rather, the bank makes sure its "backline" works harder for customers. Job descriptions for teller managers have been revised, among other things making them responsible for the front side of the teller counter, managing lines and ensuring quick transactions. They walk the floor, answer customer questions and open teller windows on busy days.

Similarly, Hardee's trains its managers to get out front with customers—literally. When a customer has a problem or question, the typical response used to be for the manager to stay behind the counter with the frontline worker. But from the customer's vantage point, that looks like a two-on-one mismatch. Now Hardee's trains its managers to walk around to the customer side of the counter, getting "up close and personal" to make the system work in satisfying ways.

Chapter 3

Process Quality

UNDERSTANDING QUALITY MEANS UNDERSTANDING that everything is a process, a series of identifiable, manageable steps that combine to make a product or deliver a service for a customer. In the words of Dr. Rodney Dueck, a physician who has brought quality tools to hospital administration, "You don't improve quality in general. You improve quality *in specific.*"

21 / Chart Your Process

22 / Chart Your Time

23 / Use Zero-Based Processing

24 / Be A Dweeb

25 / Process The Moments Of Truth

26 / Manage The Moments Of Truth

27 / Change Processes, Not People

28 / Waiting Is Waste

29 / Don't Underestimate Murphy

30 / Keep Standards Visible

Chart Your Process

TIME WAS, YOU'D START A NEW JOB AND BE SHOWN exactly where you "sat," both in the workplace and on the organizational chart. In today's process-focused, quality-conscious companies, with their interdepartmental, cross-functional teams, people may move with their work and an organizational chart simply can't show how work gets done. To show people where they're at, create a process chart. First, pencil in the major types of processes that occur in the organization. Then break each one down into the crucial details, outlining who gets what work done when, where the component pieces and parts come from, and where they go next.

With a process chart as a job aid to guide decision making, virtually any employee can fit smoothly into a new team position. Likewise, managers can quickly see when processes become too intricate and involved. Charting processes instead of people also removes the stigma (and motivational problems) involved in having some people at the "bottom" of the chart, literally under others.

Chart Your Time

HOW MANY HOURS A DAY DO YOU SPEND ON THE phone? How many minutes vanish in waiting for meetings to start, or tying up loose ends after they end? How long does it take to write a memo or call report, update a client file, fill out necessary departmental report forms? If you don't know, you're working blind when it comes to trying to improve the various simultaneous and often overlapping processes that make up your work day.

To "see" where your time goes, make it visible. Log your day in meaningful increments (half an hour max if you're doing it on paper, as little as six minutes —a tenth of an hour—if you have a computerized program to assist you). Then collate in terms of specific tasks, clients, activities and administrative time. Public relations firms often set a standard of 60% to 70% for "billable" time: Time devoted to taking care of client business. Time and motion studies, on the other hand, show the average person is productive only four hours out of eight. Where do you stand? Where do you want to be?

Use Zero-Based Processing

FROM A FINANCIAL PERSPECTIVE, ZERO-BASED BUDGET-
ing means that instead of renewing budgets each year,
often with automatic incremental increases, everything
should be rejustified from the first dollar. The exercise
is a proven way to spot fat, refocus priorities and eliminate programs that have long since outlived their use-
fulness. Why not apply it to your processes?

One company discovered 34 separate steps and
authorizations were needed to cut the check for its annual United Way contribution. The redesigned process
had four steps. What does the "process map" look like
for each of the various tasks—especially the mundane
ones you take for granted—that fill up your day and
the days of those around you? How many people touch
each part, each piece of paper? How many of them really have to? Each redundant or nonproductive step
you can identify and eliminate frees up valuable time
with which someone can do something else, improving
overall productivity as well as the specific process.

Be A Dweeb

AT BUSINESS INCENTIVES, A MINNEAPOLIS-BASED performance program supplier, a DWeeB is a Dumb Work Buster. And a hero. People at every level of the organization are encouraged, recognized and rewarded for spotting "dumb work"—work that serves no useful purpose or can be done better in other ways—and figuring out ways to eliminate it. They revel in their Dweebishness.

Dumb work can come in myriad forms. Forms, for example, that take on a life of their own long after their original useful purpose has faded. And multi-step processes that can be simplified, streamlined and made more consistent and reliable by eliminating wasteful, redundant or pointless steps. In fact, once your people start looking for it, they'll help you find elements of dumb work in everything from the layout of the office to the inner workings of the computer system, extra tasks added to already overextended people to make-work projects designed to fill out the day for the less than fully employed. Eliminate dumb work and you're working smarter. That's the point.

Process The Moments Of Truth

QUALITY TALKS IN TERMS OF PROCESS: UNDERSTANDING
the work we do as a process leading toward a desired
outcome. And continuous process improvement. Service (which is what 75% to 80% of us actually do for
a living) focuses on "moments of truth"—those in-
stances where customers come into contact with the organization somewhere during the process and have a
chance to judge the quality of what is or isn't happening on their behalf. How do you connect the two? Use
the moments of truth to plot your service delivery
process from the customers' viewpoint.

Service expert Ron Zemke describes the resulting
process diagram as a "cycle of service," a typically
cyclical series of steps that begins when customers per-
ceive a need you can fulfill and ends when they go
away satisfied (or dissatisfied). Each step in that
process is an attack point for continuous improvement
of service quality. And each may, in turn, be the pivot
point for an internal service cycle that supports and
contributes to external quality.

Manage The Moments Of Truth

JUST AS IDENTIFYING THE MOMENTS OF TRUTH CAN make the service delivery process visible — and hence subject to systematic quality improvement — it also can provide a context for measuring customer satisfaction. But while it's important to measure as a means of guiding your efforts to improve the process, it's also important to measure the right things.

According to service quality expert Len Berry, customers judge your quality from three perspectives: their initial pre-purchase needs and expectations, their personal outcome or experience, and their *observations* of the process of getting from one to the other. Whether or not you satisfy their needs, you can lose them if you fail to properly identify, respond to and manage their accompanying expectations. A technically accurate haircut performed by a rude, unwashed, clumsy barber or beautician is no more satisfying than a poor "do" rendered by someone who looks the part. Saturn auto dealerships post the real price of the car and sell it for that price, based on research that says most car-buyers resent the flea market processes of the typical show-room. How you do what you do counts, too.

Change Processes, Not People

TO BECOME MORE EFFICIENT, MANY COMPANIES "SPEED up the line." They assume if people work harder, they'll get more product for the money, more customers for the dollar. But the legacy of sweatshop approaches is often poor workmanship, high absenteeism and turnover, low morale—and customers who sense they're doing business with people who are "just going through the motions." Boosting quotas doesn't make a process more efficient. Instead of changing people, try changing the procedures they use. Let the product or service drive the process.

At Yellow Freight System, supervisors used to push workers to hustle when loads had to be moved from one truck to another. Now they park trailers with contents that need transferring *next to each other* instead of at opposite ends of a long loading dock. Burroughs-Wellcome once sifted through years of research and thousands of compounds to find a new pharmaceutical product, which then had to be approved. These days, researchers work toward specific targets and keep FDA requirements current throughout the process, making better use of both time and research dollars.

Waiting Is Waste

THE SHORTER THE SPREAD FROM THE BEGINNING OF A project until its delivery, the more likely the result is to be satisfying to the customer and profitable to the provider. A 1991 *Business Week* supplement on quality cites an Arthur Andersen & Co. rule of thumb: Product cycles that take a third of the time that competitors' take will earn three times the profits and triple growth.

How can you "speed up the line" without reducing quality or burning people out? Look for the spots where something—a part or a report . . . or a customer—sits and waits. That dead time is time that a valuable asset is doing nothing. What's more, eliminating waiting time has ripple effects that can be felt up and down the line. That's what just-in-time (JIT) processes are all about. Don't just look at lopping out a few minutes or hours: Apply zero-based processing to every stop, step or stage. Is the step itself, not just the waiting involved in it, really necessary? If not, eliminate it entirely.

Don't Underestimate Murphy

MURPHY'S LAW IS DEEPLY ROOTED IN QUALITY—OR THE lack thereof. No matter how "obvious" or "logical" something may seem, someone somewhere will surely find a way to goof it up. In Japanese manufacturing, the response is called *poka-yoke*, a wonderfully positive-sounding euphemism for idiot-proofing the processes by which work gets done.

It's easy to see the application in manufacturing: computer cables with an odd number of pin connections so the hook-up can only be made one way; tools laid out in the order of their use. But *poka-yoke* can also be applied to services and internal processes—by designing computer screens that prompt operators through the proper sequence; by laying out forms so information need only be collected once; by providing job aids, from poster-scale photos and diagrams to wallet-size reference cards, that reinforce what to do, and how to do it, and in what order or with what outcome in mind.

Keep Standards Visible

QUALITY ISN'T JUST A MATTER OF ABSTRACT PROCESS maps, run charts and statistical analysis. The more positive you can make it, the more your people can keep their actions on track. In Chi-Chi's Mexican restaurants, customer comment cards—the good ones and the ones with a refried bone to pick—are posted right above the counter where waiters and waitresses (we refuse to call them "waitrons") pick up their orders. It's a simple way to reinforce the point that the meals being delivered now will earn their own reviews.

In Pizza Huts, back in the kitchen where the customer seldom is more than a low rumble from the dining room, specific problem-solution job aids make the quality connection constantly visible. Under a headline urging pizza-makers to "Distribute Thawed Toppings Evenly," for example, is a simple equation: a picture of a poorly prepared pie in the familiar circle with a slash through it and a picture of a smiling customer, no slash. "No Center Loading, No Frozen Toppings," reads the legend to the left; on the right, "Thoroughly Coated Pizzas, Happy Satisfied Customers."

Chapter 4

Set A Quality Strategy

IN *SERVICE AMERICA*, KARL ALBRECHT AND RON ZEMKE offer a conceptual model for doing business in the "new economy"—a triangle that places the customer on the inside, surrounded by interlocking strategies, systems and people. We've adapted the model to quality, beginning with strategy considerations: Knowing what it is you're really in business to do.

31 / Use Quality As A Common Bond

32 / Benchmark Against The Best

33 / Benchmark Internally

34 / Bust The Benchmark

35 / Break The Frame

36 / Choose Your Partners

37 / Certify Vendor Quality

38 / Become A Qualified Vendor

39 / Give Your Own Quality Award

40 / Start Over

Use Quality As A Common Bond

FOR NEARLY 50 YEARS, W. EDWARDS DEMING HAS BEEN pointing out the folly of relying on the lowest bidder. If cost is your only imperative, all you're doing is driving your vendors to find ways to cut corners on quality to meet your financial targets. That's nothing more than a "limbo contest"—lining up potentially valuable allies to see how low they can go. The consequences of that single-minded fixation are writ large throughout the U.S. economy today.

In the analysis of Frank Voehl of Strategy Inc., Coral Gables, FL, "capturing the customer's voice" means making customers active partners in long-term relationships that are mutually advantageous. Whether you're the vendor or the vendee in such a relationship, there's no better vernacular than quality. If they talk Juran, learn Juran. If they construct "houses of quality," study the architecture involved. Use mutual continuous quality improvement as the common denominator that can get you beyond the immediate selfish preoccupations to efforts that link and integrate and lead to long-term stability and profitability.

Benchmark Against The Best

ONE OF THE BEST WAYS TO IMPROVE IS TO LEARN FROM those with a well-deserved reputation for quality. Benchmarking is a tactic that becomes more valuable as it becomes more specific. You don't have to become Federal Express. You just want to know how it does something you also have to do: How does it track every package in transit—in real time? How does Nordstrom inspire all those legendary stories of outstanding service? How does Apple Computer keep system designs and technical support so user-friendly?

Set your sights high: Don't benchmark against a company in the middle of the pack—unless mediocrity is the objective of your strategic plan. And be creative in selecting a benchmark. When Xerox wanted to improve the quality of its distribution operations, it chose to benchmark with L.L. Bean. Although their businesses were very different, their distribution challenges were similar, and Bean was clearly doing it better. If you're going to benchmark for excellent quality, pick an excellent model, one that will make you stretch.

Benchmark Internally

YOU MAY KNOW WHAT YOU WANT FROM CONTINUOUS quality improvement activities, but do you know if you're getting it? At Westinghouse Electric Corp., internal departments can request a week-long confidential audit that benchmarks their operations against other parts of the company. A specially trained staff measures and makes recommendations based on 12 Conditions of Excellence that range from customer orientation and human resources excellence to product/process leadership . . . and management leadership.

Westinghouse began building the function in 1985 with an eye toward emphasizing the diversity of issues involved in its quality movement while helping ensure that all departments maintain a consistent quality outlook. Like the Baldrige Award criteria, the Conditions of Excellence are flexible enough to take all operations into account, yet rigid enough to ensure corporate standards are maintained. And it apparently works: The company's Commercial Nuclear Fuels Division won the Baldrige after going through the internal review.

Bust The Benchmark

THE DRAWBACK TO BENCHMARKING IS THAT, BY DEFINI-
tion, you're following someone who got there first. No
matter how ambitious the target your benchmarkee
creates for you, you're not boldly going where no organization has gone before. That way lies what the
Japanese refer to as the "innovator's profit" — the
powerful financial and marketplace advantage that
comes from being the first to bring a new innovation
into a competitive venue.

According to Peter Drucker, Japanese firms consider money spent developing a new product or
process "sunk cost," not "investment" to be recovered
over the lifetime of that product or process. They want
to get there—wherever *there* is—first. For that reason, from the very first day a new product or service
comes to market, they start working on a deadline for
abandoning it and moving to something measurably
different and better. Try that mindset on for size.
Benchmarking can help you catch up. It can never lead
you to the breakthroughs that put you out in front.

Break The Frame

EVERY BUSINESS INEVITABLY BECOMES CONFINED BY a "frame of reference"—the way it looks at itself, what it does, what it can and should be. The frame tells you where you are. But it also can limit the way you look at what you can do. Breaking the frame means shedding some comfortable restraints and asking yourself, as service consultant Chip Bell advises, "How would [name a terrific company in a totally different field or industry] set itself up to do what we do?"

From that you get hospitals looking at Domino's Pizza for ways to cut waiting time in the emergency room. And Southwest Airlines, which has learned to treat its planes with both the TLC and the speed of an Indianapolis pit crew. Southwest doesn't offer a lot of frills, doesn't trade luggage with other airlines, doesn't serve cocktails in flight. Speed is its specialty. When it discovered that, just like every other airline, it averaged 45 minutes to turn a plane around at the gate, it could have been satisfied. It wasn't. Instead, based on studies of how Indy 500 pit crews maximize speed without sacrificing safety, Southwest now shoots for an average of 15 minutes to—safely—turn its vehicles around.

Choose Your Partners

JAPANESE BUSINESSES ARE RENOWNED FOR THEIR CLOSE, stable working relationships. Rather than shopping around for a new partner every time a new wrinkle occurs to someone, they build continuing relationships where the lines between supplier and customer become virtually meaningless. The objective is mutual advantage, even in high-tech areas where trade secrecy and protection of intellectual property have huge consequences. It's sometimes called an "open kimono" relationship—an image that speaks volumes about priorities, values . . . and trust.

It can happen here. Witness the close relationship between IBM and 3M in the continuing development of IBM's tape storage systems for mainframe computers and LANs. In 1989, 3M (which makes tape cartridges, including the kind used in the IBM systems) bought IBM's tape facility in Tucson, AZ, and kept many of Big Blue's people in place. Within two years, the partnership led to a new product with double the capacity of the old one.

Certify Vendor Quality

VERY FEW BUSINESSES OPERATE INDEPENDENTLY TODAY. The rule of thumb is interlocking business-to-business relationships through which companies sell to (and often simultaneously buy from) other companies, not end users in the consumer sense. That means the quality of the product or service *your* customer receives will be influenced by the companies you choose to do business with. It also means the quality problems those companies cause will be laid on your doorstep. Your customer expects you to be the court of last resort for quality.

That being the case, don't leave it up to your customers to tell you when something you're providing is of substandard quality. That's your responsibility. Take it seriously. For your customer's sake, and for the competitive sanity of your vendors, define the quality standards you require. In detail. In depth. In real world terms. And don't accept the idea of an "acceptable" level of failures if your customers won't. Even if 99.9% of all landings at Chicago's O'Hare International Airport are "acceptable," two landings a day won't be. Do you want to be on those flights?

Become A Qualified Vendor

IF YOU'RE SERIOUS ABOUT QUALITY AS YOUR CUSTOMER defines it, then take your *customer's* standards of quality to heart and make them basic to your own operations. Baldrige winners Wallace Co. and Globe Metallurgical willingly concede that the impetus for their quality movements came from the absolute necessity of meeting vendor certification requirements from some of their most important customers—just to retain those customers' business.

If that means taming Europe's budding ISO 9000 bureaucracy, or putting yourself through the Baldrige regimen at your customer's behest, do it now instead of later. It may well be the difference between being perceived as a proactive pioneer or a late 20th century Luddite where quality is concerned. The point is competitive advantage. No matter how limited, or limiting, you consider the proposed criteria or framework, the end objective is to further cement a valuable relationship. If, in the process, you can educate your customers to your own standards of quality—which, as it turns out, are even *higher* than those they propose—so much the better.

Give Your Own Quality Award

THE OLDEST AXIOM OF MOTIVATION IS, "WHAT GETS rewarded gets repeated." Who says the Baldrige, or Japan's Deming Prize, is the be-all and end-all when it comes to quality recognition? If quality is what the customer says it is, then you, as a customer of other businesses (and your own people), have every reason to celebrate outstanding quality when you receive it, whether internally or externally. To make it real, make it tangible.

In the aftermath of receiving the Baldrige Award in 1990, IBM's Rochester, MN, facility did exactly this. Now its annual Vendor Quality Award recognizes and reinforces the importance of the quality products and services provided to it—and, through it, to its customers—by the many subcontractor companies on which it relies. Don't just base your award on the calendar, though that's probably the most convenient way to set things up initially. The point is to never let the opportunity pass. Whether you're honoring bedrock vendors whose quality contributions are basic to your own success, or star performers in your own organization, let them know you consider their performance to be of truly award-winning proportions.

Start Over

WHEN LOU SCHULTZ, PRESIDENT OF PROCESS MANAGE-
ment International, a Minneapolis-based quality consulting firm that follows the trail blazed by W.
Edwards Deming, took his management committee on
a retreat in 1992, he didn't know he'd be reinventing
the company. But when the group couldn't agree on
the direction the firm should be taking, Schultz was in-
spired to suggest that they simply start over. Each person was asked to decide what he or she felt was best
for the company's future and all of the ideas were discussed, analyzed and merged into a consensus for what
PMI could and should become. The result was a new
organizational model—and a highly motivated staff
that knew its ideas were the basis on which future operations would be developed.

If you can't disband and reorganize in practice,
try it in theory. Start over, hypothetically firing everyone (including top management), leaving the old plant
or old base of operations behind, and rehiring and re-
building from scratch. Who and what would you
change? Who or what would you make better use of?
Then ask yourself whether you can't move toward the
same objectives in less draconian ways.

CHAPTER 5

Take A Systematic Approach

SYSTEMS ARE HOW A BUSINESS ALLOCATES RESOURCES to accomplish its strategic objectives. Over time, systems have a tendency to become outdated and unresponsive if they're not kept in constant tune. That doesn't mean having the fanciest new technology or the most elegant flowchart designs. It means what you have and how you use it should be driven by customer-focused quality.

41 / Use Technology To Its Fullest

42 / Low Tech Is Good Tech, Too

43 / Get Small

44 / Get Large

45 / Answer The Phone In Three Rings

46 / Don't Answer The Phone In Three Rings

47 / Put Customer Information At Their Fingertips

48 / Use The Sorry System

49 / Recover Systematically

50 / Empower Within Boundaries

Use Technology To Its Fullest

SOME OF THE MOST CRUCIAL QUALITY CHALLENGES ARE right under your nose: the electronic servants on which your business increasingly depends. Yet most businesses use only a fraction of the capability built into their systems. That's waste. Set time aside to learn the basic functions and fancier bells and whistles available in your computer, your telephone, your facsimile machine, your photocopier, your presentation aids. Develop your own quick-reference job aids to make lesser-used hardware and software functions more memorable and productive. Share copies with others on your team.

If that means jettisoning some outdated macho baggage, so much the better. Don't hold onto the "good old days" for nostalgia's sake. Once we prided ourselves on brawn. Now we measure brainpower—both human and electronic. Technology creates new opportunities, new capabilities, new and more productive ways of doing old jobs. When that takes some of the grunt out of the work, it lets people concentrate on the quality-centered aspects of their tasks. Or do you really want to trade today's computers for manual typewriters and carbon paper?

Low Tech Is Good Tech, Too

NOT ALL TECH IS HIGH-TECH. BUT ANY TECH THAT HELPS improve the quality, consistency and efficiency of a system is good tech—whether it plugs into a grounded outlet or not. You can "process data" with a clipboard and a #2 pencil; the task doesn't require a laptop computer with a 40-megabyte hard drive. If a broom with an angled handle improves cleaning efficiency and reduces back strain, it can be as good an investment in cleaning technology as a mechanical floor sweeper with rally stripes and digital monitoring.

At GTE Lighting, a major, yet elementary, switch in the manufacturing process saves more than $8,000 every time a machine is reset. Instead of requiring employees to manually measure parts and materials, simple gauges and stops have been installed on machines. Now measurements are both faster and more consistent, giving the customer a higher quality product for less money and allowing workers to do their jobs in significantly less time.

Get Small

TOO OFTEN, WE STILL SUFFER FROM AN EDIFICE COM-
plex: "My building is bigger than your building, so my
company must be better than your company." Wrong.
Bigger isn't better. *Better* is better. And in a business
world where quality service is a driving force, more
companies are finding that smaller is better: A network
of decentralized regional offices or niche-focused service teams often satisfies customer needs far better than
one large complex organization replete with 19 levels
of bureaucracy.

The American Automobile Association (AAA) is
actually an association of associations: more than 150
locally chartered and operated clubs that tailor services
to specific regional needs. IDS, one of the brighter stars
in the American Express constellation, runs every regional office as an individual profit center, funneling all
services through them and allowing each to handle its
own staffing needs. To make good on its guarantee of
48-hour, zero-defects check printing, Deluxe Corp.
routes work to more than 60 close-to-the-customer
plants coast to coast.

Get Large

THERE'S NOTHING WRONG WITH CENTRALIZATION that improves quality. In 1988, Northwest Airlines ranked 12th out of 14 carriers in on-time arrivals. Its computer system was fragmented—operators sometimes needed several keyboards and monitors to fully access and display flight, routing, weather and other information—and the people who used the system were scattered among 14 departments in three separate buildings. No more.

Northwest put the computers and the people who relied on them in one operations center and backed them with upgraded technology. Now 400 dispatchers, aircraft routers, meteorologists and others involved in daily operations can access anything from time-lapse satellite weather data to the exact location of each plane, airborne or on the ground. Quality improvements range from faster decision making, which can help keep flights on schedule, to the ability to route planes around turbulence in mid-flight, giving passengers a smoother and safer ride. And the bottom line? Northwest expects its $6.5 million investment to result in savings of $9.4 million. Annually.

Answer The Phone In Three Rings

OR TWO RINGS. OR FOUR RINGS. THE POINT IS NOT THE number. The point is that the longer you keep customers, internal or external, waiting, the more time and goodwill you waste. Setting a definite target for answering the phone gives everyone a standard for the important process of telephone answering. But to be useful and valuable, that standard should be more than arbitrary. And recognize that if staffing and equipment aren't adequate to handle the volume in the time targeted, frustrations will grow and morale will drop exponentially.

At AMP, the international manufacturer of electronic connectors and components based in Harrisburg, PA, the customer service center answers the phone on the *first* ring. AMP's research shows that as many as eight callers out of 100 will hang up if their calls aren't answered by the third ring (about 14 seconds). To drive that number down below one percent means answering calls in five to six seconds. Because there's proven value in capturing those calls, AMP targets that strenuous standard—and deploys systems and staff accordingly.

Don't Answer The Phone In Three Rings

FROM THE CRADLE, WE'VE BEEN TAUGHT THAT A RINGing telephone *must* be answered. Adding an element of scorekeeping suspense only further reinforces what is sometimes a bad habit. For example, when a person who is already working one-on-one with a customer has to (or chooses to) stop the transaction in progress to answer a phone call, the message communicated to the first customer is loud and irritatingly clear: "Wait your turn, Bub. This phone call may be more important than you are. And even if it isn't, you can wait, but it can't."

Modern telecommunications technology offers tremendous potential. Misused, misdesigned or misdirected, it offers tremendous jeopardy for customer relationships, internal and external. Systems are servants, not masters. Your people should be supported with high quality systems that help them help their customers—and management, training and team support to handle the phone when they can't. And if you're using, or considering, one of those technically intricate, multiple-menu call management systems that routes people through an electronic Skinner box of button-pushing, you'd better find out how your customers expect you to react when your phone rings.

Put Customer Information At Their Fingertips

MINNEAPOLIS-BASED TENNANT COMPANY'S CUSTOMER service reps handle an average of more than 30 calls a day apiece. They can provide direct, personalized responses to each customer's needs because of a highly sophisticated computer system that lets them call up virtually any piece of information about the client relationship: the machines each owns, account activity, service and volume, purchasing agreements, customized pricing structures, credit levels and other variables.

The integrated system also tells them what products are in the warehouse and which are on trucks at any given moment. It allows them to walk customers through diagnostic trails on every product Tennant sells or has sold, or proceed immediately to a three-way conference call with a technical support person. Good data system design and management not only saves time, resulting in more productive service reps, it means more satisfied customers because service needs are handled by people who can do what needs to be done on the first call.

Use The Sorry System

LOOKING FOR A PLACE WHERE YOU'RE LIKELY TO GET plenty of bang for your continuous quality improvement buck? Listen for two magic words: "I'm sorry." What do your people constantly end up apologizing for? Every time they tell a customer, internal or external, they're sorry, they're providing a tip-off to problem quality areas, showing you a potentially powerful place to spot consistent fail points and an equally powerful starting point for using the Shewhart cycle (Plan-Do-Check-Act) to design customer-pleasing solutions.

As the Shewhart cycle cautions, don't just jump in. Former newsman Eric Sevareid is remembered for the tart observation now known as Sevareid's Law: "The chief cause of problems is solutions." Make sure you know what's going wrong, why it's wrong (from the *customer's* point of view), what employees involved believe accounts for the continuing nature of the problem, and what the consequences of your remedial actions may be.

Recover Systematically

DON'T BEGRUDGE PEOPLE THEIR "I'M SORRY" OPPORTU-
nities. According to service quality experts Ron Zemke
and Chip Bell, the process of *recovery*—literally return-
ing your customer to a healthy, pre-problem state—can
not only undo the damage of a transaction gone bad
but actually build greater loyalty than what you'll find
among those who pronounce themselves satisfied.

Recovery, say Zemke and Bell, properly begins
with an apology, an admission by the provider of the
service or the deliverer of the product that the quality
experienced by the customer was not up to snuff. The
next step: listen. Let customers tell you in their own
words what they thought they should have gotten vs.
what they did, and what might make things right. Then
take care of both—the problem and the customer.
Sometimes, "symbolic atonement" (a coupon, rebate or
other tangible symbol of your continuing interest in their
business) is in order. Then, for the icing on the cake, follow up: Get back in touch in a few weeks or months and
make sure they're happy with your response.

Empower Within Boundaries

ONE OF THE BIGGEST BUZZWORDS OF THE QUALITY movement, *empowerment* has fostered its share of confusion as well as commitment. Some organizations fear the very idea because they think it means anarchy: Giving people the power to do anything at all. Not so. In the words of Joel Smith, a consultant with Wisconsin-based Joiner Associates, a quality consulting firm, empowerment means "you have the authority, responsibility and accountability to handle your job as defined *in the system*. But you must stay within the confines of things you can get your arms around."

Western Merchandisers, a division of Wal-Mart that distributes books, videotapes and records, creates a working definition of this systematic vision by training employees to understand what they can and can't do to solve specific customer problems. A minor complaint, for example, can see the customer receive a coupon for a free movie rental or a free drink at the snack bar. It's left up to the employee to decide what's most appropriate within those boundaries; the system of boundaries narrows the options toward appropriate solutions.

Chapter 6

People Make It Happen

NO MATTER HOW TARGETED THE STRATEGY, NO MATTER how smooth-running the systems, a business' quality quotient is no greater than its people. Selected properly, trained intensively and extensively, empowered to act toward quality outcomes, and recognized and rewarded for getting it right—for the business and for the customer—people create world-class quality.

51 / Hire The Best

52 / Recruit

53 / Use Employee Differences

54 / Create Quality Folklore

55 / Emphasize Personal Purpose

56 / Set Empowering Goals

57 / Reward Quality

58 / Evaluate Compensation

59 / Support Your People

60 / Manage People For The Long Term

Hire The Best

IT SOUNDS ELEMENTARY. BUT SOME COMPANIES GET SO busy filling slots on a corporate position chart that they forget those people are individuals who will be dealing with customers, whether internal or external, one-on-one. Under the pressure of getting the work *out* the door, they hire the first people *in* the door who meet the minimum requirements. That tendency is only heightened when the jobs in question are less desirable entry-level positions.

Whether the job is to work on a production line, deal with customers or manage employees, a body is not just a body in a quality-conscious company. Disney conducts at least two separate interviews (involving two different interviewers) with each person it hires. At the Honda plant in Marysville, OH, management long ago made a conscious decision to hire only the best employees, often extending searches well past the old norm, interviewing several times, if necessary, for any job, and waiting for top-quality people to walk through the door. The result? Today, word has gotten around that Honda is looking for good workers—and an average of 200 people apply for each job.

Recruit

DON'T WAIT FOR GOOD PEOPLE TO FIND YOU. LOOK FOR them. Constantly. Personally. And through everyone in your work group. Carry a pocketful of business cards and make a point of giving one to people, wherever and however you happen to meet them, if they seem like they could play well on your team. Encourage your people to do the same. Hospitals responded to the nation's nursing shortage by paying bounties, not just to new hires, but to the staff nurses who encouraged them to apply. At Stew Leonard's famed Connecticut dairy store, about half of the 700 people on the payroll are related to someone else on the payroll. Stew uses nepotism instead of forbidding it. He figures work ethics run in the family.

Remember to help your recruits work their way through your company's procedural maze. Don't assume the folks in Personnel know what you need or want. They know how to comply with the myriad laws and policies that govern hiring, and they're specialists at screening and processing. But only you can tell them about the working environment in which your new hires will have to survive and thrive.

Use Employee Differences

ONE PLACE ANY QUALITY MOVEMENT SHOULD ACTIVELY seek variation is in its workforce. Instead of being expected to conform to neat little boxes that correspond to bland job titles, employees at quality-conscious companies are more likely to have a closet filled with corporate "hats" they can don at will to help fill any number of roles on any number of problem-solving or service-giving teams. Chosen well, those hats reflect not only job functions, but people's unique capabilities.

When Cadillac switched its design structure to simultaneous engineering teams—people are assigned to small work groups that regularly discuss their participation in the total process, anticipating how one functional area will affect the others—women on one team were insistent that glove compartments be redesigned so they could be opened without damaging fingernails. It's a little thing, something Cadillac's male engineers say they never would have considered. But it's also something women, as customers, appreciate as quality.

Create Quality Folklore

PEOPLE DON'T IMMEDIATELY UNDERSTAND AND embrace a quality-oriented corporate culture. For continuous comprehension as well as continuous improvement, quality messages must be consistent, simple and clear from the beginning, showing exactly what the company wants, but in very specific settings. Abstract concepts are fine as far as they go. But they seldom go far enough. The human side of quality thrives on anecdotal evidence: stories that illustrate quality in action and offer role models so people can better understand what quality "looks like" when they're getting it right.

Make your quality folklore rich and diverse. At Aerojet Electrosystems, a regular newsletter tells stories that show quality in action. But instead of the usual corporate platitudes so common in house organs, Aerojet's newsletter features employees who go above and beyond the call of their job to improve quality, whether in large ways or small. The division president also hosts quarterly luncheons to personally thank people for their contributions.

Emphasize Personal Purpose

EMPLOYEES WHO TAKE PERSONAL OWNERSHIP OF THEIR work, who have an opportunity to "leave fingerprints" on even the most generic of products or processes, are highly motivated to put the quality touch into everything they do. Their name on the product means the product is an extension of their effort, often their personality. Ask a Federal Express employee—at any level—why the percentage of packages delivered on time and intact is the best, and you'll hear, "We have to be perfect. We deliver the most precious packages in the world." That's purpose.

Purpose can be reinforced through personal touches as simple as making sure everyone who needs, wants or can use one has a name tag and business card. Managers and other paper pushers find they're more motivated if they're allowed to sign the reports they've worked on. Manufacturing firms in industries from clothing to industrial machine tools include a note with the inspector's full name, not just a number. Marlin Guns engraves the technician's name onto the firearm itself. Personalize your quality.

Set Empowering Goals

NOT EVERY EMPLOYEE'S JOB LENDS ITSELF TO DISCOVERing constant improvements or going all-out to meet customer needs. And even those who constantly make measurable improvements may need corporate approval (in essence, the permission to take on new tasks and the protection to keep working at them if the results don't match the initial expectations) before they feel empowered to tackle a time-intensive effort or a complex project that requires enlisting the support of people in other departments.

Chevron motivates employees to pursue longerterm, inter-disciplinary projects with "stretch goals," a quality-focused variation on the management by objectives theme. Working with their supervisors, people not only set goals that go beyond the basic job description, they receive top-level approval to develop their own teams from across the corporation as well as set time limits and other standards for measuring success. By making "stretch goals" mandatory, Chevron forces people to break out of their neat little job boxes and make quality a pervasive force companywide.

Reward Quality

AT LANSDOWNE CONFERENCE RESORT IN LEESBURG, VA, employees know what their bosses think is a good job because, whenever they're "caught" going above and beyond for the customer, they immediately receive a card that can be traded for the chance to win prizes. At the Sheraton New Orleans, convention groups pass along Mardi Gras-style doubloons to specific staffers who help them. Northwest Airlines gives some frequent flyers special cards that they, in turn, can give to flight attendants and others who make their travels more enjoyable; the cards can be turned in for various premiums.

Reward efforts don't have to be relegated only to measurable successes. One way to motivate people in internal jobs is to ask them what they're proud of. Plan periodic bragging meetings. Encourage people to constantly tell others thanks, both through formal memos as well as informal chats. Post positive letters around the office. Mary Kay Ash, the founder of Mary Kay Cosmetics, has turned the simple act of praise into a multi-million-dollar business: "We praise people to success," she says.

Evaluate Compensation

PREDICTION: COMPENSATION IS GOING TO BECOME ONE of the stickiest issues in the quality movement. When employees go above and beyond, pushing quality and performance to ever-higher levels, and taking on increasing amounts of responsibility once jealously guarded as the turf of their managers, they certainly can't be faulted for feeling they should be rewarded accordingly. But when the job description says they're *supposed* to go above and beyond at every opportunity, what can you do?

"Pay for knowledge" systems are one option. Individual team members at Aid Association for Lutherans receive base pay for the primary services they perform and additional pay for new skills learned and applied. At Shell Oil's Sarnia, Ontario, plant, pay scales in the unionized shop are based on each employee's job knowledge as determined by peers. People receive the higher compensation even if they rarely use the additional knowledge — management figures smarter workers bring more to the table and help solve problems faster.

Support Your People

DEMOTIVATORS, DISTRACTIONS AND DISRUPTIONS COME in as many shapes and sizes as employees themselves. And with today's increasingly complicated lifestyles, the personal issues employees bring to work can consume more energy than the job itself. The need for flexible hours and reliable daycare, the need to leave work early to care for sick children or attend a school event, the needs of a spouse's career can all cause productivity-reducing personal stress and produce ripple effects for others on the team.

At Patagonia, the Ventura, CA-based garment manufacturer, happy employees are a goal, and the company virtually stops at nothing to achieve it. Benefits include on-site kindergarten and daycare, generous parental and health benefits, subsidized wilderness adventures as well as employee discounts that are 10 percent below wholesale. The daycare center alone stops five to 10 people a year from quitting, figures CEO Yvon Chouinard. Multiply that by the average $50,000 it takes to bring a new worker to peak efficiency, and he figures the generous benefits are a good investment. His workers agree.

Manage People For The Long Term

EMPLOYEES ARE AN INVESTMENT IN THE FUTURE. THE quality-conscious company knows it's true. We've all heard the stories of entrepreneurs such as Seymour Cray, who, fed up with the computer company he was working for, quit and founded Cray Research, the world-renowned supercomputer design firm (a company he has now left to start *another* new firm). Likewise, the late Sam Walton went into business for himself because his former management wouldn't let him expand a small string of five-and-dime stores fast enough. His "I can do it better myself" idea: Wal-Mart. What might the original companies have become if they'd said "yes you can" instead of "don't bother us"?

Instead of making them quit in frustration, allow your own forward thinkers to become *intrapreneurs.* Let them set aside a portion of their time to work on a project their own way. Lend a supportive ear to the products of their basement tinkering or after-hours "skunk works." That's the underlying philosophy that led to 3M's Post-it notes, McDonald's Big Mac and the powerful financial projections tool now used at Blue Cross-Blue Shield.

CHAPTER 7

Learn Quality

MORE THAN HALF THE JOBS WE DO TODAY REQUIRE training beyond that we receive in the traditional education system. Competitors from Germany and France to Japan and Korea are putting their smartest technology in the hands of ever smarter workers. If continuous *process* improvement is a watchword of quality, continuous *people* improvement merits a similar priority.

61 / Train Initially

62 / Spend 12 Days On The Train

63 / Put Quality On The Agenda

64 / Reinforce Basic Skills

65 / Teach The Business

66 / Cross-Train For Quality

67 / Nurture Soft Skills

68 / Learn Customer Needs Personally

69 / Learn From The Competition

70 / Build Some Fun Into Learning

Train Initially

QUALITY-CONSCIOUS EMPLOYEES ARE CREATED, NOT found. People need a basic grounding in quality ideas and tools before they can begin to use the concepts of continuous improvement, empowerment and effective problem solving. Anytime you add someone new, make sure they have a practical background in quality: the concepts, the tools, the accomplishments in businesses from Japan to down the block. And that's just for starters.

Even quality experts can't know exactly how to put the basic concepts immediately to work in your unique business setting. Specific application principles should be the second part of every employee's initiation. At Patagonia, new employees attend a two-day, 12-hour quality course in their first 90 days. The course introduces them to the teachings of such quality gurus as Philip Crosby and W. Edwards Deming, then details exactly how to solve problems within Patagonia's corporate culture. They learn from day one what Patagonia expects and how they can contribute to the company's success.

Spend 12 Days On The Train

FRANK VOEHL, WHO CUT HIS TEETH ON QUALITY AT Florida Power and Light, the only U.S. company to earn Japan's respected Deming Prize, heads Strategy Inc., Coral Gables, FL. He argues that training has to be a deliberate strategy of personal and personnel improvement, not a half-hearted use of leftover time. And while good training, like good medicine, is as much a matter of quality than quantity, he offers a basic guideline for those who need a starting point: 12 days a year, budgeted, on the clock, for everyone.

Not practical? Not possible? Sound like a prohibitively expensive investment? Then consider that 12 training days a year is the equivalent of two training hours a week. Or less than half an hour a *day*. As the Romans knew, *divide et impera*: divide and conquer. Mix longer, more intensive training sessions for larger skill-building needs with a variety of brief, to-the-point, action-oriented sessions. But make sure you actually do them. Support continuous improvement with continuous learning.

Put Quality On The Agenda

ONE OF THE AGE-OLD TRAPS OF FORMALIZED LEARNING is seeing it only as a "down from the mountain" process: Assuming that knowledge can—indeed must—only be imparted by accredited authority figures whose wisdom surpasses the understanding of mere mortals. There's a need for that kind of expertise, to be sure. But there's also a lot of common sense resident between the ears of your people. Tapping it not only informs and improves others, it also affirms, reinforces and reenergizes people who sense that their experience and accomplishments are truly valued by the organization.

At Disney's theme parks, in the regional operating centers of American Express, in countless offices, restaurants and manufacturing facilities, people increasingly are being asked to help train each other. They get together regularly, sometimes with a structured agenda (pick one quality concept or tool a month to explore or review), sometimes just to talk shop, but always to continuously improve their own quality efforts.

64

Reinforce Basic Skills

FROM MEDICINE AND REAL ESTATE TO THE AIRLINES and nuclear power plants, continuing education is increasingly the norm. Sometimes that's because "the knowledge" changes. Sometimes it's because it doesn't. Every six months, Federal Express drivers must pass a written test on the company's service strategy and the skills involved in their role in it. Supervisors must pass the same test. By continually reinforcing the basic skills and their relevance to the task at hand, FedEx not only ensures they become second nature, but reminds everyone that customer-focused quality comes before everything else.

Training doesn't end when everyone officially knows their jobs, or when they've passed a test, or when they're promoted to management's ranks. When the customer is the most important variable in the business equation, basic frontline skills are the most important variable in the employee equation. Even the smoothest-running quality machine can stand a periodic tune-up.

Teach The Business

IN TOO MANY COMPANIES, RESIDENTS OF THE BOARD room barely know where the frontline is and the frontline is expected to mindlessly worship the supposed knowledge sitting in the plush chairs surrounding the mahogany table. There's a recipe for quality disaster. At Springfield Remanufacturing Center Corp. in Springfield, MO, open-book management is now the norm. Workers on the line are taught to understand the effects of costs and revenues, strategic goals and departmental productivity on their jobs. And executives are expected to know the nitty gritty of how the company serves and satisfies its customers.

Nothing is more empowering than knowledge. Taking the mystery out of management builds true frontline respect for the decisions executives must make. Knowing what's really happening at the frontline makes those decisions more practical and effective, less abstract and omniscient. The interplay nurtures teamwork and buy-in, especially when people are being asked to change processes and procedures they've lived with for years.

66

Cross-Train For Quality

CHECK INTO THE UNIVERSITY PLACE CONFERENCE CENTER and Hotel in Indianapolis and you may find a chef at the front desk, a housekeeper in the kitchen, a front desk worker making beds. They're cross-training, expanding their skills, their knowledge of the organization and their job horizons. At Neles-Jamesbury, cross-training is the rule: This Worcester, MA, valve manufacturer has collapsed 120 job titles into seven broad categories and trained its workers to move readily among a wide variety of duties.

No matter how you approach it, cross-training can reap big benefits. By looking at jobs through different eyes, people often find new solutions to old problems. They're more understanding when something goes wrong in another department, and can automatically pitch in when someone is sick or when there's an emergency, no matter whose organizational turf it involves. Because they know a variety of jobs well, they're quicker to solve a problem today instead of passing the buck to someone else.

67

Nurture Soft Skills

WHEN MINNESOTA-BASED ZYTEC CORP. BEGAN HIRING employees for its electronic power supply manufacturing plant in the outstate town of Redwood Falls, it attracted many middle-aged, first-time job holders. They were fully capable of doing the shop tasks, the "hard skills." But before they could accept the responsibility of empowerment that went with them, Zytec found they needed organizational and communications skills, too. So the company provided "soft skills" training in such areas as dealing with conflict, problem solving, team building, personal responsibility and communicating nondefensively. It also organized classes in which team members, long accustomed to working alone, could learn to trust each other and see the value of working together.

The result of such "ego-building" training: This 1991 Baldrige Award winner was able to eliminate product inspections while simultaneously decreasing the percentage of defective product because instead of deferring to inspectors, all employees commit to working together to do their jobs as perfectly as possible.

Learn Customer Needs Personally

HOW CAN YOU IMPROVE QUALITY IF YOU DON'T KNOW who it's for? At Dun & Bradstreet, the customer is identified by asking two questions: Where does my work go? Who is it important to? People who understand where their work goes, and that it's appreciated, are more motivated to produce a quality product every time, whether the customer they're serving is on the outside or sits just down the hall.

Remember that customers are people. For behind-the-scenes managers or production workers who rarely leave the factory floor, customer data in the form of one more impersonal report or another staff meeting can fade quickly. Medtronic brings in the recipients of its pacemakers and other lifesaving medical implants, both literally and figuratively. Yearly meetings feature everyday people telling workers how the products they make have helped them live to see their children grow up or made their lives pain-free. Throughout the year, letters and photos from people whose lives were extended and improved because factory workers did their jobs right are posted on special bulletin boards. People know *that's* where their work goes. *That's* who it's important to.

Learn From The Competition

WITH THE HIGHEST SALES PER SQUARE FOOT IN THE industry, Stew Leonard's Dairy Store in Norwalk, CT, has become a mecca for businesses trying to improve their retailing quality. But being the best means constantly being ready to change, so periodically a half dozen or so Stew Leonard employees pile into a van or station wagon and head off to a competitor's location (with nearly 100 food retailers in a 15-minute drive radius, there's no shortage of places to go). Once there, they're expected to check out how the competition's doing and come back with at least one idea for improving the way Stew's takes care of its own business.

Scouting out the competition is a simple but effective form of product and process training—and a valuable type of competitive research that costs virtually nothing to conduct. Your customers have plenty of alternatives, no matter what product or service you provide. View the competition from the customer's vantage point and you'll "see" how you compare. You also might learn a thing or two.

70

Build Some Fun Into Learning

SKILL-BUILDING IS AN ESSENTIAL PART OF EVERY QUALITY effort; products and services are only as good as the people providing them. Even entry-level employees feel pride if they know they're good at something. And that same pride can make anyone an even better service provider, people manager or problem solver.

But continually teaching and reinforcing basic skills to long-term employees can become pure drudgery to everyone involved. Solution? Domino's Pizza makes it a game. To build pride and professionalism in its varied workforce, the company's annual Pizza Olympics gives employees from throughout the company a chance to compete for awards that are coveted for the prestige of being proclaimed the best of the best. Semi-truck drivers negotiate an obstacle course. Frontline employees are purposely harassed in phone calls, then judged on how they handle the inevitable "customer from hell." Cooks make huge amounts of dough and turn it into pizza crusts. Everyone laughs a lot—and goes back to work focused on improving their performance next year.

CHAPTER 8

Communicate Quality

IN BUSINESS, ABSENCE DOESN'T MAKE THE HEART grow fonder. No news isn't good news. Business relationships thrive on constant communications—communications that will be all the more effective if they're planned, conducted, checked and reviewed in keeping with an underlying quality imperative. What kind of quality messages are you really sending?

Do It Externally

TREAT ALL FORMS OF COMMUNICATION AS FORMS OF *marketing* communication: From bills and forms to advertising and sales literature, they should be designed for the positive role they can play in showcasing your quality to your customers. Are your messages clear, consistent and customer-focused? Are bills and invoices accurate and easy to understand? Can customers decipher product literature and technical manuals, warranty statements and service policies? What does your correspondence say about the quality of the business they've chosen to do business with?

Make your messages both easy to obtain and easy to understand. Don't use 250 prolix words where 25 will do, nor begrudge 250 well-chosen ones just because 25 are more cost-effective to reproduce. Choose the words carefully. Spell the words correctly. Make the pictures and diagrams truly helpful, not just eye candy. If you take communications for granted, you miss the chance to reinforce the reasons your current customers chose you and prospective customers should.

Do It Internally, Too

WE ONCE SAW A PHOTO IN AN EMPLOYEE NEWSLETTER that showed several executives (in *de rigeur* suits and ties) with several production line employees (in coveralls). The "suits" were identified by name, the line workers weren't. Message: Executives are important: real people with real names; frontline folk aren't. Ouch! How you say what you say says a lot about your commitment to quality. You wouldn't cheapen the quality of customer tangibles—not just the product, but the packaging and accompanying support materials. Why do the equivalent internally?

Spiff up employee communications at every level, including those the line-level people originate. When UPS frontliners in the company's KORE (Keeping Our Reputation for Excellence) program present their work group results, they use the same slides, overheads and laser pointers common in higher-level meetings. If they need help preparing those materials, they get it. Message: These results are important and should be communicated as effectively as any other information in the organization.

Keep No Secrets

LIFE INVOLVES GOOD NEWS AND BAD NEWS. BUSINESS IS
no exception. If you and your customers are managing
relationships for the long-term, you have to trust that
you both have the maturity to deal with the ups and
downs. Don't fear sharing good information within a
quality relationship, whether the customer is external or
internal. People need to know where they stand and how
they're doing, especially when they're doing well. By the
same token, don't bury or fudge the bad news. Serve it
up straight and focus on the continuous improvements
indicated, not who should get blamed for what.

Hal Rosenbluth, CEO of Rosenbluth Travel in
Philadelphia, invites every employee to schedule a day
to tag along with him, promising only the most confidential information will be kept from them. At U.S.
Healthcare, an electronic "vital signs" board in the re-
ception area flashes the organization's score on a variety of key service measures for all to see: how fast
phones are answered, claim-processing speed, how fast
membership materials are getting to customers, even
overall corporate attendance.

Advertise Your Quality

CAREFULLY. CONSISTENTLY. AND ACCURATELY. CADILLAC did the Baldrige process—and itself—a disservice by trivializing years of sustained quality improvement efforts for a brief bump in its consumer advertising. People don't buy cars because the company that made them won an award for something. They buy cars that meet their needs and expectations for a car. That the cars on the showroom floor have been improved because of a long-term continuous improvement process that is still evolving is too complex a message for today's manic 15- and 30-second advertising spots. All that came through was, "We have two-door, four-door and *quality* models this year."

On the other hand, Deluxe Corp., the nation's largest printer of checks and other financial forms, puts its quality standards (48-hour turnaround on orders, each printed with zero defects the first time) and its annual performance against those standards in each year's annual report. Presented in their proper context, quality messages help create and manage valid quality expectations.

Encourage Quality Feedback

NO ONE KNOWS WHAT YOUR CUSTOMERS WANT BETTER than your customers. Yet too often businesses get caught up in trying to second guess what "the market" wants, spending thousands of dollars and waiting months for the results of big, supposedly definitive surveys, focus groups and other high-level research instruments. Obviously, there's value in that kind of information. But there's also gold to be mined from the specific, personalized feedback your customers can offer individually. Encourage it. Acknowledge it. Listen to it. And share what you hear with others throughout your organization, especially at the frontlines.

Some companies take the quest for customer feedback a step farther. Medtronic, noted for its pacemakers and other implantable devices, recruits customers—physicians and surgeons from around the country—as product advisors. It credits their direct involvement for faster product improvements, continuous steps crucial for creating greater quality for the end-user patient as well as enhancing long-term customer loyalty in general.

Provide Quality Feedback

AMERICAN BUSINESSES SEEKING TO ENTER JAPANESE markets often are confounded by obstacles, both visible and invisible. While eliminating or overcoming overt trade barriers is clearly an issue, the more significant part of the challenge may actually be breaking into the collegial working relationships that have matured over decades among Japanese companies. You don't look for new vendors if you're intensely satisfied with the quality, reliability and sweat equity in the relationships you've developed with companies you've worked with for years.

What is a major challenge abroad can be a powerful asset closer to home. Building solid, stable working relationships helps both partners. And the glue that holds the relationship together is a two-way, constant flow of information and feedback. To get constantly improving quality from your vendors, provide a constant stream of constructive feedback on how well (or poorly) they are meeting your needs and expectations. Use the feedback channels they provide for you, and seek others if you feel there's mutual benefit in a still larger flow of information.

Improve Your Technical Literature

SINCE REDUCING VARIATION IN THE PROCESS OF MAKING A product or delivering a service can improve quality, shouldn't the same dynamic force be applied to what happens to it once it's in the customer's hands? The best-designed electronic marvel, the best-delivered medicine or law or consulting counsel can fail to meet customers' needs if those customers don't know how to get full value from whatever it is they've purchased from you.

That doesn't just mean producing a hefty manual to tell them "everything they need to know." Good information is helpful, understandable and presented in a user-friendly way. The first thing savvy computer users do when acquiring a new software package is buy a user's guide that will be more functional, not to mention more understandable, than the documentation packed in with the disks. Self-help publishing ranges from the basic (health care, how to build and sustain relationships, financial planning) to the arcane—evidence that people want and need more information on the products and services on which they depend.

Resist Wretched Rhetoric

IF YOU'RE FOLLOWING DEMING'S 14 POINTS, THIS COMES with #10. Quality isn't a political campaign. Don't treat it like one. American business is renowned for its love of "flavor of the month" programs that are launched with great fanfare but quickly fade as top-level interest and commitment wanes, only to be replaced by a new program when something different strikes an executive's fancy. Programs start—and end. *Continuous* quality improvement is a process. This one doesn't get over.

So get real, especially in how you communicate your quality standards. The customer, for example, is not always right. Research shows about 30% of the problems a given company has to solve will be caused by its customers. Experience confirms that every day for people at the frontline. If the customer's always right, and something goes wrong (as it inevitably will—read up on normal and abnormal cause, or our old friend Murphy), your people can do the relevant math pretty quickly. They'll work industriously to cover up the problem instead of exposing it and risk getting blamed for it.

Cascade The Message

THE TRICKLE-DOWN THEORY HAS TO BE ALIVE AND WELL in American business, if for no other reason than that corporate cultures are top-down in nature. Consequently, whether it's a new twist on a statistical tool or a fundamental change in corporate mindset, most organizations find the best success from "cascading" information: starting the communication flow from the top and reaching each successive level in its turn (eliminating layers and levels obviously results in a faster information flow).

At Motorola, the cascading of quality information started several years before the Six Sigma philosophy became part of the overall corporate culture. Top executives first had to be convinced they had to find a new way of doing business; courses on such top-level topics as "Winning Globally" and "Asia: Past, Present and Future" built that understanding. From there, each level received quality training in its turn, assuring that managers fully understood the tools to be used and the theory behind Six Sigma before helping their employees learn and use these skills.

Six Sigma Your Communications

A HIGH SCHOOL TEACHER (AN ENGLISH TEACHER, NO less) once confided that he and his colleagues ignored the poor spelling, grammar and syntax of their students lest they "inhibit creativity." True story. Horrifying story, especially since communications quality is the life's blood of modern business. It is *not* creative to have three ways to spell every word in the English language, or to be proudly ignorant of other people's customs or concerns. It's sloppy. It's ritual stupidity. And it's evidence of poor quality.

You don't have to be in manufacturing to apply Six Sigma quality. You can use the same standard on your own work processes—and very likely with visible impact. For example, if your work involves writing (whether technical reports or routine correspondence, product literature or internal materials), Motorola-style Six Sigma means you can misspell, mispunctuate or otherwise garble 3.4 words out of every million words you write (*two* per billion if you're using the pure statistical six-sigma standard, notes service quality author Grace Major). Against either of those benchmarks, what kind of quality are you communicating?

CHAPTER 9

===

Team Up For Quality

THE RHETORIC OF AMERICAN BUSINESS HAS ALWAYS borrowed a lot from the world of sports. We "win" in the marketplace. We care intensely about "who's No. 1" in our industry. We train our people and exhort each other to "keep your head in the game." Today, teamwork and coaching are tandem priorities, recognition that organizations must work *together* to succeed.

81 / Wear Your Colors

82 / Eliminate Management

83 / Coach Quality

84 / Cross Boundaries

85 / Majority Doesn't Rule

86 / Involve The Union

87 / Beware The Mack Truck

88 / Put Another Drop In The Bucket

89 / Reward Team Effort

90 / Give Teamwork Time

81

Wear Your Colors

IN THE GAMES PEOPLE PLAY, THE RULES ARE CLEAR, THE competition regulated by physical boundaries and time limits, the sides evenly matched (at least numerically), and there's a convenient scoreboard to let everyone know how they're doing. In the work people do, winners and losers are harder to identify from one moment to the next, the rules and the playing field are constantly changing, but the organization's priorities are the same: Build winning teams that can combine the individual skills and efforts of many individuals to succeed against talented competitors. And just like sports, the customer resets the scoreboard to 0-0 every day and the game begins again.

To encourage teamwork, take a page from the athletic playbook. Develop quality skills — the "fundamentals." Make sure people know how they measure up against the competition—the "scouting report." Use quality statistics as a scoreboard—it helps everybody identify "all-star" performance. Encourage camaraderie and team spirit: Think in terms of lineups and depth charts instead of organizational charts. And when you win, celebrate.

Eliminate Management

NOT MANAGERS, MANAGEMENT. BACK IN THE JUST-industrializing world of Frederick Taylor, our work processes were far more complex than our workers. His solution: Break down the process into easily doable parts and leave the coordination, trouble-shooting and decision-making to others. Today, the situation is reversed: Knowledge, experience and high-tech tools have given workers ample power to deal with even highly complex and exacting jobs. Managing is now a support function. No longer is the operative concept to monitor people as they work docilely at lockstep work-stations. Now the task is to mesh their skills and efforts into smooth-functioning teams.

Not only is this changing the way people work, it also has to change the way we manage work. When Schott Corp., a Minneapolis-based electronics manufacturer, replaced traditional plant managers with leadership teams that included one person from each of the different areas of the plant, the company saw product quality, productivity and morale improve. Teams succeed when all their players contribute, responding capably from their individual positions with purpose and proficiency.

Coach Quality

WHETHER THEY'RE ACTORS OR ATHLETES, MUSICIANS OR maestros of food or fashion, top performers have confidence in their competence. They feel they can take a risk, stretch a limit, invent a spontaneous response to an unexpected challenge. And it's the rare exception to the rule who reached that level while being held back, second-guessed and reprimanded for showing initiative and drive.

Just as there's a difference between people working alone and teamwork, there's a difference between supervising and coaching. Much of what changes is the manager's role. Once it was performance appraisal. Now it's performance improvement. Appraisal, as practiced by the traditional American business, is a disciplinary process, a way of keeping the numbers up and the people in line. Improvement is a learning process. It's driven by knowledge, not authority. Yelling at people doesn't help them improve the quality of their performance. Teaching them does. Encouraging them does. Positioning them to succeed and then letting them play the game does.

Cross Boundaries

MANAGERS HAVE KNOWLEDGE AND EXPERIENCE WITH processes and skills that apply far beyond their own basic turf. Similarly, frontline workers have knowledge and experience with processes and skills that also can be valuable when applied somewhere else in the organization. Cross-training is one way to spread them. Cross-matching can be another potent tactic, one that will not only cross-pollinate ideas, but build better functional teamwork and understanding.

To close the distance between frontline work groups and mid-level managers who have little exposure to what those groups have to work with (and through), try matching groups and managers cross-functionally. "Give" a work group on the manufacturing floor a manager from accounting (or personnel, or MIS or wherever) for five hours a month (the number is arbitrary, but pick one). "Loan" five hours a month of a plant worker's time to customer service (or sales, or R&D or wherever). Make sure the hours are accounted for, evaluated and productive—as rated by the work group. Make sure the turf travelers share what they learn, too.

Majority Doesn't Rule

ONE KEY TO BUILDING A TRUE QUALITY CULTURE IS building commitment from all corners of the organization—not only among managers, where power has traditionally resided, but even more importantly among those who for many years have been systematically disenfranchised. People unaccustomed to acting in empowered ways may need a little time to get the hang of it. And their fragile sense of involvement will be quickly broken if they are constantly overridden by management fiat or a vocal clique.

Total quality applies to everyone. That means everyone has a voice in it. Not a vote, a voice. The purpose is not to build situational majorities and play power blocks against each other, but rather to build true consensus where everyone involved sees the point of what needs to be done and contributes to getting it done. And the nay-sayers? No is never an acceptable answer. It's incumbent upon those who think a given tactic isn't the right one to help develop an alternative that is. Quality isn't some of us vs. others of us. It's all of us working together.

Involve The Union

LEONARD WOODCOCK OF THE UNITED AUTO WORKERS is remembered for observing that unions often reflect the managements with which they deal. Where relationships are strong and positive, the foundation in place will support an extensive quality structure. Where rancorous adversarial interests have been the dominant theme in labor relations, a lot of mutual remodeling is needed. The past won't be left behind quickly, no matter how many people have good intentions—or frozen smiles pasted firmly in place. But change is possible. That's a basic lesson of quality.

At Ford, at General Motors' Saturn operations, at NUMMI (New United Motor Manufacturing Inc., a joint venture between Toyota and GM), quality is not a subject for negotiations. It's a common ground on which both management and union representatives meet and work together for mutual, not selfish, advantages. That alignment leads to ripple effects that spread corporate culture change. If you assume "the union guys" (or "the guys from corporate") will automatically oppose your quality overtures, you may be right—but for the wrong reasons. Ask yourself whose agenda you're pushing: yours, theirs . . . or "*ours.*"

Beware The Mack Truck

TEAMS THRIVE ON GROUP EFFORTS. THEY FALL APART when people go off in their own separate directions or develop their own jealously guarded turf where no one else dares intrude. The consequences for the organization can be profound. If a key player on your team got hit tonight by the proverbial Mack track, would someone else even know what they were working on, let alone be able to pick up the project and see it through to completion? If not, you run the risk of losing the value of all that work in progress—plus the customer waiting for it.

Firms in law, accounting, public relations and other professional fields know the value of having backups familiar with the client; many work at being "three-deep" with key accounts. Use the same standards with your teams to avoid information monopolies that can become black holes if an individual drops out of sight. And make sure your electronic players are also "insured." Computers—and the records in them—are vulnerable to theft, fire and other disasters, natural and manmade (remember the Michelangelo virus?), as well as system failures. Back up electronic files, including software configurations, offline. And regularly.

Put Another Drop In The Bucket

WHEN THE UNIVERSITY OF PENNSYLVANIA FORMED quality teams to brainstorm ways to reduce postage costs and improve the quality of the university's mailing efforts, it turned up an interesting anomaly. Brainstorming meetings tended to spark creativity both on and off task: Some ideas the group generated fit the specific mission assigned, but other ideas, just as good, didn't apply to the subject at hand.

At first, the consensus feeling was that even recording such ideas wasted time and got people off the track. But on second thought, team members decided exactly the opposite: Good ideas were good ideas, they reasoned, and even though some didn't fit the team's own activities, that didn't mean they wouldn't help another team. So they created, figuratively speaking, "the bucket." Now, whenever a good idea pops up that might be relevant somewhere else, it gets dropped in and passed along. Kind of gives new meaning to the hallowed tradition of a bucket brigade, doesn't it?

Reward Team Effort

WITH MORE AND MORE BABY BOOMERS VYING FOR increasingly fewer management slots, the idea of team playing can run counter to career conditioning that traditionally has rewarded people individually with pay, perks and promotions. It's predictable that some will give lip service to teamwork while trying to continue their own personal climb to the top. If the organization, high-sounding rhetoric notwithstanding, continues to reward that kind of selfish behavior, teamwork is doomed.

But even the most competitive industries have found it doesn't have to be that way. At Goldman Sachs, one of the most respected firms on Wall Street, employees are evaluated for pay raises, promotions and partnership positions in part on the basis of "credit memos"—detailed recaps of a team effort that give credit wherever and to whomever it is due. Promotion is based on both those they've received and those they've *written*. Other organizations reinforce teamwork by allowing team members to share the spotlight of group successes, to determine each other's bonuses, even to approve or demur on candidates for open positions on the team.

90

Give Teamwork Time

CONSIDER EXPANSION TEAMS IN PROFESSIONAL SPORTS. They wear uniforms just like everybody else's. They play the same game everybody else is playing. They're made up of skilled professionals, many of whom once were considered all-stars or key contributors in other organizations. They're managed by experienced people who can draw on lessons learned through decades of competition. Yet most take years to become even marginal contenders for the top spots in their industries (i.e., leagues).

It takes time to meld individuals, no matter how talented, into smooth-functioning, competitive organizations. Sometimes, in fact, self-centered talent can get in the way of team development. Teamwork doesn't happen overnight—not in sports, and certainly not in a business world where team orientations are relatively new and untried. Some organizational development specialists maintain it takes a minimum of two or three years just to *begin* to make lasting changes in a corporate culture. Be patient. Quality takes time.

CHAPTER 10

Lead By Example

WITH ITS ATTENTION TO DETAIL AND ITS WORLD-CLASS vision, quality helps us link together very small, insignificant, incremental steps into a journey of near-epic proportions. That means everything counts. Everything. What you do and how you do it. What you say and what you don't say. Inevitably, the portrait of your company's quality looks like you.

91 / Develop A World View

92 / Develop A Customer Focus

93 / Learn The Language

94 / Preach What You Practice

95 / Dress For Success

96 / Remove Barriers

97 / Reinforce Quality—Quickly

98 / Criticize Constructively

99 / Stop Looking For Silver Bullets

100 / Walk The Talk

Develop A World View

THERE'S A REASON FOR THE PHRASE, "WORLD-CLASS quality." As our world becomes ever more tightly knit economically, quality concerns are increasingly transcending borders, currencies, languages and the legacies of history. It's a worldwide phenomenon. We can't ignore it. It isn't going to go away and let us go back to our old, comfortable, local ways of doing things. This is nothing less than a survival issue, personally and professionally.

Your career and your company are caught up in this swift-flowing current. You can choose to go with the flow or you can try to find yourself a backwater pool where you can hide. But don't kid yourself: Ignorance is seldom bliss. Those who, as the futurist Alvin Toffler advises in *PowerShift*, develop an ability to "learn, unlearn and relearn" will be valued for their contributions. Those who don't or won't may find themselves working for and depending on people who literally speak another language.

Develop A Customer Focus

"ANALYSIS PARALYSIS" COMES FROM BEING OVERLOADED with information that all looks alike: There's no way to distinguish the truly significant from the inconsequential. Since quality is for customers, make that your point of view. See your quality as your customers see it. Hear the customer's voice in your planning meetings. Make the customer's priorities your operational guidelines. And do it personally.

There's no one who can tell you faster what customers do and don't like about your products than a customer who's using them at the exact moment you ask. Actually seeing the interaction between your products (or services) and your customers can give you valuable insights into mismatches, shortfalls and new business opportunities as well as potential problems and possible solutions, that neither you nor your customer might have thought of in more formal settings. Jim Miller built Texas-based Miller Business Systems, an office supply dealer, into a market leader by visiting 200 customer locations a year. For 25 years.

Learn The Language

WE ONCE HEARD A MANAGER BOAST THAT HE DIDN'T know the difference between a bar chart and a scattergram, and didn't see any need to learn. Yet, he assured us, he was as "into quality" as the next guy. We doubt it. Would he trust a surgeon who said she didn't know a scalpel from a catheter, or a mechanic who seemed proud of his inability to tell the difference between a crescent wrench and a tire jack? And would he willingly (let alone confidently) follow the lead of such "leaders?"

Quality has its own distinct vocabulary, its own specific tools, its own pantheon of savants. Learn them. Teach them to others. The more everyone in your work group speaks the same language, uses the same tools, follows the same guiding principles (whichever principles you've chosen), the more consistency and cohesiveness you'll develop. Reducing variation works with the vernacular, too. The alternative is chaos, a corporate Tower of Quality Babel where the best of intentions are lost in the din.

Preach What You Practice

THE LATE SAM WALTON, WHO BUILT WAL-MART, THE nation's largest retailing company, from a chain of expanded five-and-dime stores located primarily in small towns, is remembered for more than his financial success. There also was his TGIM attitude—"Thank God It's Monday"—which aptly described his love of his life's work. For years, Walton disdained a corporate limousine for an aging pickup truck and tried to spend two or three days a week in his stores talking with his "associates," the term for employees he borrowed from J.C. Penney (his own first employer).

At Miller Business Systems, the operative word is "terrific." Ask Jim Miller, who bought the business when it was all but bankrupt and nursed it into a $150 million dollar success story, how he feels, how he's doing, how it's going, and his reply is always the same: "Terrific!" The refrain is now basic company vocabulary from the front office to the loading dock. It's not just happy talk, either. There is power in positive thinking.

Dress For Success

NEARLY A CENTURY OF OFTEN BITTERLY ADVERSARIAL labor/management relationships has given managers a deep reservoir of suspicion about people "out in the shop." It has created similar cesspools of distrust for "the suits" among those at the frontline. Quality doesn't mean that we ignore the past. To the contrary, it assumes we won't stubbornly adhere to old patterns that simply perpetuate ill will and cynicism.

If "what you see is what you get," don't hide behind false fronts. Dress—up *or* down—for success. If you're a manager, leave the suit and tie, the oxfords or high heels, the power briefcase and notebook computer back in the office when you go out to work with the frontline. If you're a frontliner, clean up your act, and yourself, before heading into the cubicle canyons far from the grit and grime of the workplace. When people make a point of looking different, all that gets noticed is "the look." Minimize style differences and you make it easier for everyone involved to focus on substance.

Remove Barriers

ARE YOUR PEOPLE GREETING PRONOUNCEMENTS OF THE quality crusade with a hard-edged cynicism? Remember that they've heard grand statements before. Now that you're trying to give them the two-edged sword of empowerment, they're acting reluctant to reach for it, perhaps for fear that it will be turned on them, perhaps as well for recognizing that they don't know how to wield it effectively. The idea of empowerment is sound. It's the "giving" metaphor that's getting in the way.

According to Chip Bell and Ron Zemke, empowerment is not a gift. It's the result of removing the barriers—the absence of permission, protection, proficiency and purpose—that keep people from acting in empowered ways. Look for the policies and procedures, the dissonant fiats and the disempowering folklore, that have been used as barriers to keep people in their place (and that they're now hiding behind). Get rid of them. They're roadblocks on the quality journey.

Reinforce Quality — Quickly

THE QUICKER YOU REINFORCE QUALITY BEHAVIORS, the quicker people—whether subordinates, colleagues or superiors—will be about making them into habits. Recognition loses its impact if it's diluted (spread among people who didn't really do anything as well as those who did), preempted (generations of managers have earned brown-nose points from *their* bosses, and the undying enmity of their subordinates, by taking personal credit for group efforts) or received too long after the performance. Like food for the body, this kind of food for the quality soul is best when it's fresh, pure and served up in satisfying portions.

So if you know it when you see it, and you see it, point it out. Caveats about sexual harassment noted, use everything from a pat on the back or a hearty handshake to a "good job" chat or "thanks for the good work" memo; a surprise donut, an impromptu lunch, a bouquet of flowers, tickets to the ball game. Don't defer to the employee of the month bureaucracy or (heaven help us) an annual performance review to tell your people they've done good. Do this job yourself. Every day.

Criticize Constructively

IF REINFORCING GOOD QUALITY IS THE UPSIDE, COMING to grips with substandard work, and workers, is the hard part. We have precious few models on which to draw. "Soft skills" like nurturing and coaching are the things we've long been taught to suspect rather than respect. Now, when we need them the most because we need our people to really get with the quality program, we're tongue-tied and still too prone to make 'em smart rather than making 'em smarter. In case there's any doubt in your mind, professional relationships bruise easily; abusing them is *never* productive in the long-run.

The trick is to separate person from performance, then focus on improving performance in ways and toward targets on which everyone can agree. UPS uses the principle of "least best," working as groups in which everyone (but some more than others) has room for improvement instead of singling any one person out. Adding balance helps, too. Maryland-based Preston Trucking transformed an intensely negative corporate culture by formalizing an expectation that managers would say *four* positive things for every *one* negative.

Stop Looking For Silver Bullets

IN THE POINTED ANALYSIS OF ANNA MARAVELAS, A Minneapolis-based quality consultant, the basic metaphor of the Lone Ranger illustrates a dysfunctional quality system. Think back to the typical exciting episode. Something bad is happening. The good but passive local townspeople know it, but they're unable or unwilling to help themselves overcome it. Then in rides the Masked Man and his Potowatomi senior assistant change agent, a few bad guys are run off or killed off, and our heroes ride off into the sunset, leaving behind a trademark you-know-what—*and people no better able to take care of themselves than before.*

Instead of waiting for silver bullets to be supplied by conveniently passing experts, recognize that you have plenty of ammunition in the people and processes all around you. Start your own quality journey by taking the initiative close to home. Those accustomed to seeing themselves as powerless will not (can not) act in empowered ways. But people who take personal responsibility for what's going on around them are using power already readily available to them. They make empowerment a buzzsaw, not a buzzword.

Walk The Talk

WILL ROGERS ONCE OBSERVED THAT PEOPLE LEARN more from observation than conversation. Your most memorable grade school teacher (or coach, or aunt, or other formative influence) probably expressed it as, "Actions speak louder than words." As Don Meredith (in the words of Dizzy Dean) told Monday Night Football viewers for years, "Sayin' it don't make it so."

However you choose to express it, it's true. Pronouncing quality isn't the same thing as practicing quality. More than what you say, your people watch what you do. And how you do it. If you can't be bothered with the picky little details, they'll do the same. If you cut corners, so will they. If you see customers as an inconvenience to be suffered through, they'll learn—and communicate—those same attitudes and behaviors. But if you make it clear, in everything you do as well as everything you say, that this quality stuff is important, they'll believe the evidence before them. The best way to lead is by example.

Have Fun

HAVING FUN ISN'T TYPICALLY A PLANNED OUTCOME (or even hoped-for byproduct) of the continuous quality improvement movement. You probably haven't seen it discussed in "the literature" or presented in keynote or breakout sessions at quality conferences.

But without it, quality is just the same old productivity squeeze with a human face. It isn't going to bridge the gaps and tear down the barriers in our workplaces: It's going to reinforce them. We already know what that feels like. We already know it leads to dysfunctional systems, noncompetitive products and services, disgruntled people—and customers looking for something better.

It doesn't have to be that way. We believe the growing focus on quality is once again giving people the chance to leave fingerprints. That alone can be a critical element in restoring a sense of purpose, pride, satisfaction and, yes, enjoyment, to the work we do.

Think about the idea of fingerprints for a moment. Over the past hundred years or so, we've "lost our hands"—lost our ability to physically touch our work in ways that once made it a reflection of our own personal pride and commitment. Where once we did things or made things as hardy individuals, or extended families, or close-knit guilds, now we find ourselves caught up in huge impersonal systems against whose scale and scope we seem to pale into insignificance. This is not just a manufacturing phenomenon. The same malaise is deeply ingrained in educational institutions and government agencies, group medical practices and group-think professional service firms, grocery stores and car dealerships, banks and airlines.

That's the BIG PICTURE. And you can have it.

Pursuing TOTAL QUALITY encourages us all to think small again—to reach out to the parts of the process or the product that we can personally touch and control and effect and leave our fingerprints all over them. This is no place for the elegant or the aloof, the pretentious technocrat or the nitpicky bureaucrat. Continuous quality improvement means getting our hands dirty again, getting down off our high horse and walking right in at ground level, playing in the workplace mud if that's what it takes to make it or do it better for the customer.

Don't kid yourself: That's change on a dramatic scale from the way we've been doing business. For generations now, in the vernacular of careerism, you learned to get ahead in business by "climbing the ladder." In the typical business, the power, the perks, the prestige, the pay all get better as you work your way higher and higher on the organizational chart. And how do you do that? By turning your back on the customer and getting just as far from the frontlines as you can contrive. Everybody knows nothing good happens to you down there!

It shows. People who don't enjoy what they're doing, who don't think it's important or valued, simply don't do it as well as they can. They overlook the key little details that make the difference between okay and outstanding. They let things slide, figuring somebody else will clean up after them. They keep closer tabs on the clock than on their work. They figure quality is someone else's job.

We didn't get into this mess by accident. We worked our way into the swamp. And we can work our way out. Trouble is, we're prone to make things far too hard for ourselves. You leave fingerprints today the same way you did when you were five years old: Once you get your hands dirty, you touch places where you can leave an impression. And in its own strange way, this form of quality function deployment feels just like it did when we were five—like we're getting away with something. After all the years of seeing our efforts sanitized for someone else's protection, of seeing every last vestige of personal contribution erased in the supposed grander cause of Acme Ajax Amalgamated, quality is virtually mandating that we regain the use of our own hands . . . and it feels *good*.

For people who have been waiting a long, long time for the chance to feel good about what they do, this looks an awful lot like fun.

We think it's about time.